enjoy this book. Please return or
You can renew it at
or by using our free
one

and

D0774392

After . . .

The Impact of Child Abuse

ROBINSON

First published in Great Britain in 2019 by Robinson

Copyright © Libby Moore, 2019

Illustrations by Tony Husband

1 3 5 7 9 10 8 6 4 2

A CIP catalogue record for this book is available from the British Library.

ISBN: 978-1-47214-425-6

Designed by Design 23

Printed and bound in China by C&C Offset Printing Co., Ltd.

Papers used by Robinson are from well-managed forests and other responsible sources.

Robinson
An imprint of
Little, Brown Book Group
Carmelite House
50 Victoria Embankment
London EC4Y 0DZ
An Hachette UK Company
www.hachette.co.uk
www.littlebrown.co.uk

After . . .

The Impact of Child Abuse

LIBBY MOORE
Illustrated by Tony Husband

ROBINSON

INTRODUCTION

My name is Libby Moore, and as a little girl I was sexually abused.
This has had a major impact on my life in so many ways. The abuse
experienced by little me continues to affect big me, so I decided
to go back and meet that little girl, to connect with her, to
understand her and to understand what happened to us.
Here is our journey.

Oh no, please not again . . .

Oh . . . who are you?

Don't worry. I'm you, grown up.

I don't understand. How can you be me?

Come with me. Let me explain . . .

I want to talk about the things that are happening to you . . . to us.

Look! Can I have a milkshake?

4

I play over there on the swings, but I don't know this place.

Yes, it's quite new. You won't have seen it yet.

Can we talk?

About the bad things? It's so scary, though.

Wow! Long time, no see. Still looking gorgeous!

Erm . . . thank you.

7

He made me jump!

Oh sorry, did he? I jump easily too.

8

Move over, sweetie. Let me give you a cuddle.

Ugh . . . oh . . .

It's when he wakes me suddenly . . . it's frightening, so I jump.

Yes, of course – that's where it comes from.

What's he doing? I don't like him.

Oh dear. Take no notice – he's harmless.

No, he's not harmless, he's horrid like him.

I know, I know he is . . . why don't you tell our family about him?

12

Because he's always nice to me when anyone's around.

And he's a man and I'm just a little girl.
Why would they believe me?

It makes me so angry. He's destroying *us*. I've got no self-esteem.

What's self-esteem?

Having no self-esteem means that when you look at your reflection, what you see is worthless . . . meaningless.

How I feel about myself affects my day-to-day life so much. I'm petrified of public speaking . . . I imagine they are mocking me, laughing at me . . . it's horrible.

But they're not, they're really enjoying it.

I keep doing it, though – beating myself up and
punishing myself with anxiety and doubt.

I can't take any criticism, and I'm scared of standing up for myself in case I offend someone.

Your report is full of mistakes.

Oh, is it? I'll redo it, sorry.

Then I get angry with myself because he's putting me down and I don't do anything about it.

But do you know what I'd love to do?

No, what?

Go back in and and stand up for myself.

23

Actually, this report just needed a few tweaks.
I think you'll see it's fine now.

OK, thank you, I'll take another look . . .

But I never do. I lie awake for hours, tossing
and turning, calling myself names.
I don't believe in me.
I'm scared.

That's sad. Can't you talk to anyone?

Oh, I have. I've had lots of help and support.
I've had counselling . . .

I want to find the 'inner me' that feels so lost.

. . . talking in groups is very reassuring in that
I feel I'm not alone . . .

. . . I've tried relaxation techniques and
given myself quiet times to reflect . . .

. . . it all works for a while but . . .

He's hurting us, isn't he?

He is. He really is. Have you tried asking
him to stop?

He scares me too much. I can't.

I feel like it's *me* being bad. He tells me that it's OK, that it's our secret, and not to tell anyone.

It's so wrong. He's controlling you – me – it never stops,
even now I'm older. I allow other people to control me.

But I told you I didn't want to go! OK, OK . . . I'll get ready. No, of course, I don't want to let people down.

I feel like everyone is more attractive – and better – than me.

I feel so sick inside when
I look at myself.

I can't respond intimately.

I can't look into anyone's eyes. My eyes
dart around all over the place.

Perhaps I'm scared they might see little you
deep inside, lost and ashamed?

40

I'm so sorry that he's taken your innocence
and your trust.

I know why you turn your eyes away when you're talking to someone, by the way.

Why?

Because that's what I do when he does those things
to me. I can't look him in the eyes, so I turn away.

Yes, of course. How awful for you,
little one.

Ah, still here! Fancy coming back to mine for a . . . *drink*?

Oh! No thanks, I'm busy.

Oh, come on. Let's see that sexy body of yours in action!

Erm, no, sorry. I'd best get on . . .

Your loss, darlin'. Anyway, call me sometime. See ya.

Uh, yes, OK, I will. Bye.

He's horrid. Why do you let him talk
to you like that?

I don't know. I know it's wrong, I do.

Then get up and tell him! You shouldn't let anyone
speak to you like that.

You're right. I will.

Excuse me, can I have a word?

Oh, wow! Changed your mind, then?

No, I haven't. How dare you speak to me like that?
How dare you abuse me in that way? Don't ever speak
to me again, understand?

Right . . . OK . . . got to go . . .

I did it! I stood up for myself!

You did! You were so cool!

Come on, let's walk to the lake. I love it there.

I spend hours here. It's so peaceful.

I'm not allowed here on my own. I'm too little.

I'm glad you came to find me. Care about me, won't you?

I will, little one, I promise.

I love you.

I love you too.

Take care, little one.

Resources

If you are concerned that a child is being sexually abused, or if you are an adult survivor of childhood sexual abuse, there are national organisations and charities that can offer support and guidance.

These are just some of the organisations to offer advice:

Barnardo's	www.barnardos.org.uk
Family Matters	www.familymattersuk.org
Moodswings	www.moodswings.org.uk
One in Four	www.oneinfour.org.uk
Rape Crisis	www.rapecrisis.org.uk
Safeline	www.safeline.org.uk
Save the Children	www.savethechildren.org.uk
The Lucy Faithfull Foundation	www.lucyfaithfull.org.uk
The National Association for People Abused in Childhood (NAPAC)	www.napac.org.uk
The National Society for the Prevention of Cruelty to Children (NSPCC)	www.nspcc.org.uk
The Survivors Trust	www.thesurvivorstrust.org
Women's Aid	www.womensaid.org.uk